PANNING GOLD

FINNS WAY BOOKS POETRY SERIES
Kathleen Stamm, Editor

PANNING GOLD

Patrick Stevens

FINNS WAY BOOKS

Published by Finns Way Books
Oakland, California

Manufactured in the United State of America

ISBN 978-0-9985288-8-5

To four of my closest friends: Sharon, Catherine, Jackie, and Kath, whose encouragement kept me writing and helped me reconnect with the days of my youth.

In the end, old friends are the best friends.

CONTENTS

III BECOMING (cont.)

IV DISTANCE

PANNING GOLD

Panning Gold

Patrick Stevens

I

REMEMBRANCE

I

REMEMBRANCE

Panning for Gold

Rest.
Consider the life I've lead.
Dreams rushing back,
moments I lived but had forgotten.

Gold.
Brilliant, flecks flipping
past in a fast-flowing stream.
little gems lost.
Now recovered.
I grab a pan and sluice the sand.

Old Uncle Vern bouncing and swaying,
playing his pedal organ in that house on
Coffee Lake before it burned down.
A thrill of happy dance music
played with such zeal on a sunny afternoon
with all us kids dancing silly,
such fun.

Grab a pan and sluice the sand.

We
walking hand in hand
down that cool morning May path
off into the woods by Maki's field,
sneaking a little kiss to warm the air,
tall grasses ruffle apart,
there a newborn fawn lay

hid, alone quivering alive.
We hush walked by
hush walk by.

Grab a pan and sluice the sand.

The pillow raft that on my bedroom floor;
an isle amongst thrashing 'gators
we fought, bravely fought,
brother Tom and I
always beat them back.
Fought and won as the sunrise brought
full light to the room's gloom.
The sounds of a coffee pot perking
made us shake the dust out
of the pillowcase and
jump back into bed, warm.

Grab a pan and sluice the sand.

Watch the sparkles rushing past
on a dark dim morning.
I, an old man, waiting sunrise,
thinking a life through to pose:
What was it all worth?
Where did it go?

It is not the gain; not what wealth can sate
but the gleaming gems,

the rare loving glimpses of memory
making a clear path ahead.
It is who I become when the lights dim
and all around me the dark paces in.

Grab a pan and sluice the sand.

REFLECTION

In my life
every dawn was a new door.
Soft wind ruffled curtains
hung to hide morning's light,
but I greeted the breeze,
happy to see
another sun risen.
To hear again
that rust hinged screen door
rattle squeak,
looking out to see
past a gate across our drive
where a field danced
with sharptailed grouse
in midair,
like spirit birds,
through heavy morning fog
formal and proud.
We too danced
the morning air.

In my life
storms cracked the sky
above that little pond
out back where cattails grew,
and we skated in winter,
roasting marshmallows,
over coals of a woodfire,
midnight on its shore,

cold night air
settling around us,
huddled blowing away the flame,
waiting to cool the crust down.

In my life
we were never so cold
though the coals were dim,
never shivered.
Always my days were
filled with flowers,
bright spring blooms,
and pretty, kind ladies and gents
dressed in their summer best,
wearing those white cotton gloves,
veiled sun bonnets,
fedoras, jackets and ties.
You don't see that
much at all anymore;
all proper and elegant
at a time
when flowers and kindness
still persisted after the war.
They are still there
where I left them
just last night.

In my life
I have seen beauty

and touched love to my lips.
I have heard mourning doves
coo hoo, coo hoo. at sunset.
All that matters
is the elegance,
the certainty, and respect.

Knowing all is well
for yet another day.
It is as if
I am a skipped stone
on calm waters.
The splash and rings
winding out across
a still, mirrored,
crystal universe.
l stand here
at a new door
waiting it to open.

WE ARE THE POETS

We are the poets
with large hearts,
busy building rainbows
to carry all our words forward
toward those generations
those whose minds
hold spears and lances
and mouths are filled with dust.

We are the poets
connecting stars,
rising with the moon,
and setting the sun.
Seeing constellations
within and without
our stirred souls.

We are the poets.
Builders
of myth and reality
tomorrow's truth told today
for the ages far
away we cast into
the pool of the future
sometimes catching a nice fat trout
or angry eelpout.
The cast still the same.

We are the poets
whose very words
lifted all humanity from the mud
off slimy cave bottoms;
who drew icons to tell all
where to find the food
to chase the game
to feed the family of man.

We are the poets,
strong and alive,
carrying words of power
across all the generations
through all of the nations and people
in every language 'til today,
where we drag the past on into tomorrow.

II

COMMUNITY

CLOQUET, MINNESOTA: 1954

In those days
the town worked.
We worked all we knew
recycling pop bottles.
repairing shoes
making paper, toothpicks
insulation, milled lumber
selling what we had
to whom we knew.
The town worked.

I suppose you'd recall
that pop bottling shop
down behind the V.F.W. on tenth and main
right across from S&L dry goods
and that little shoemaker's shop
to the rear where the German worked
to re-sole and repair
worn out work boots and shoes
back when every man in town
either worked, or had worked,
in a mill or the forest,
and most of the women too.

Good pay for a day's work
running three shifts
day in and day out
every day of my young life;
all day long

steam switch engines ran the tracks
below the avenue
Chug….chug….chug
Huff, huff, huff, huff
like the impaired breath
of an old set of lungs,
sucking in slowly
then puffing out
Chug….chug….chug,
Huffhuffhuffhuff
All day all night long,
All day all night long.

The bottling shop
guys would pay
four cents a bottle for regular,
clear glass washed pop bottles, or
five for those green tinged cokes.
An easy fortune on a summer day
for two eight-year-old kids
looking to make pocket change
to buy a candy bar, or root beer to share,
or maybe a movie at the theater
right across the avenue.
who knew?
so Charlie and I, we'd
scoured the streets in the neighborhood
looking for empties

here and there...
sometimes hitting gold, sometimes not.
but worth a shot, why not?

And sometimes we'd just hang
outside the bottling plant
 to see the bottles whir through the machine
filling and capping, filling and capping
the glass bottles clinking, tinkling,
as they rolled by on the belt
filled and crated
one end to the other
orange, strawberry, root beer, grape
an endless afternoon cycle
on a hot summer day
 each new flavor
a delicious odor.
moist and rich
washing out the garage doorway
out onto the street.

In those days
the town worked.
we worked all we knew
recycling pop bottles.
repairing shoes
making paper, toothpicks
insulation, milled lumber

selling what we had
to whom we knew.
The town worked.

JUST LIKE HOME

Greek John's gone.
His fortress fry grill
wrecked, replaced
by a fast gas, neon lit
station store
where wandering folks from
all forty-eight contiguous states
wheel through a familiar
big city plot right there
where was John's shop.

Feeling, I suppose,
like they've seen some piece
of a small town America.
Folks are friendly here,
Thank you, mam,
Isn't it just like home?

Now buried
those polished oak wood walls,
counter tops bruised with dust and age
lying lost in the county land fill
no longer reflect
me and my buddies
sucking down our cherry/lime cokes
ducking to sneak a smoke,
while Greek John,
his white aproned shape,
jabbered on the dark side of the

fountain grill,
filling our greasy orders out.

Crowded into steamy booths
carving initials of
our loves,
our hopes,
and dreams.
Blasting our way through top twenty
chart busters,
strutting our stuff.

Or earlier cruising loud into
our place,
to rest after a long night's carouse,
filtering past the dusty shelves
we'd browse
for a Zippo, or Dutch Master,
or skin magazine
trying to find some action,
seeking the answers that
Greek John guarded
like gold.
his treasured backroom tales.
He sold us our age,
no more.

John's bus stop shop's
been genericized

into the same neon glitter
we see on T.V.
so wandering folks
from all forty-eight contiguous states
wheel through this familiar
city plot here where,

Greek John's gone.
The past ever perfect removed
by bulldozer blades.
our merry dim spot diminished,
but fast
here resting still where
no dust filtered sun light pierces.
His empty shelves, bereaved.
Greek John's gone.

FIVE AND DIME

In Ben Franklin's store,
up near the front,
(so that old biddy clerk could spy
what a boy was up to),
were wooden bins
set on the first aisle shelves
lined up the hardwood stripped floor,
where you could stand
near eye level,
tip toed, and see
piled in a heap

(Don't touch!)

hundreds
of little khaki colored, plastic men
dressed as soldiers
holding rifles posed to shoot,
or standing at attention,
some marching ahead,
lying prone pointing
guns held tight
enemy in sight.
Oh, which to buy!
kapow, kaboom

(Put that down!)

all just a couple inches
of cheap Japanese plastic.
Made to make
the mind of a boy spin
war out of his dreams
on the bedroom floor before
the folks got up
early in the morning
light

(No loitering!)

or afternoons out in the
backyard sand box
where Pa's midnight shift
banished all friends away
a boy played outside ,
where a small,
quiet war could be fought
by the general and his troops
kapow, the rifle,
kaboom, a grenade
a rattaatat of machine guns
tanks rattling around
and little plastic men
falling, *oof,*
all through an afternoon
while Pa slept

and mother
made the evening meal

(That will be ten cents, young man.)

all ready for a war
fought before I was born
there on my bedroom floor
with rugs as barricades,
miniature tanks charging,
the huns and the ruskie commie dogs
breaking through my side
I always won my war.

July Fourth

Just fifty-five years past
this date fired my eyes.
The world a wondrous place,
my little town by the river
filled with all the people
of all Carlton Country
for our great celebration
of the founding of our nation,
and carnies and fireworks
and a parade and the fair.

We snuck firecrackers and cherry bombs
We ate itty-bitty doughnuts.
Cotton candy stuck to our cheeks.
We played silly games of chance
and lost our small change,
again and again.

We thought of hot summer love;
watched shouting crowds stroll past
in tight laughing groups
to crowd Pinehurst park
as we spun tilt-a-whirling
long into the night.

July fourth was the best summer day ever.
It will always be.
My arm around the waist of my first,
my only love,

sitting on the hill
on a blanket above the ball field
where the fireworks boomed high
so bright and flashing.
Boom aboom boom.
The stars lying behind.
I remember stars lying behind.

A hot night ahead
and all the world forever a dream
in my sixteen year old head
there where my life began
fifty-five years past.

SUMMER NIGHT

On my block
the game was kick the can,
every summer night
until bats whirled,
the sun dimmed down.
kick the can,
shouting,
kick the can.
never, ever
wanting to be it
for that last kicked can
because Ma said be home by dark
and it was getting near dark,
best run.

Playing with Trains

We played with trains
in hot mayjune.
Big switchers pulled
loads in and out
on the winding tracks
down behind Grandma's house
there on Avenue C
where we sat on grey rock perches
in tall dry grass and watched
the huge engines chuff by.

One day with penny in hand
we waited for a switcher
to start running the yards
chugging cars and cars and cars
first this way,
then that
on this and that track,
banging and booming,
back and forth on those hard steel rails.

With a single penny we conducted
a small experiment to see
how flat railroad wheels could smush
a thin copper coin
as they rode the rail by.
Flat, flatter,
hot and huge.
We grinned.

Another day, tipping rocks,
we found a garter snake nest,
writhing with fingerlings,
and trapped one for us
to take home in a jar
filled with pulled dry grass
huddled home in a jar.

Where an encyclopedia
would allow us to know
what a snake ate,
where it needed to live,
how it might survive,
so we could give it
a life in our own.
tiny snake zoo.

But more to the point,
(more often than not)
Ma caught us sneaking
in through the back door
just as she did with all the other
frogs and toads and odd bugs
we dragged home
and made us
take that poor snake back,
and turn it lose,
for God's sake, right

back where we found it
down under that rock
behind Grandma's house
there on Avenue C
where we played with trains.

Trapping the D. M. & I. R.

An old, abandoned rail yard stretched
north on the St. Louis River,
just across from Dunlap Island
and the balsam wool plant
hooting and spewing
steam on a cold winter morning
years gone by
years gone by.

There was nothing of work life
left in the yards,
a double set of railroad tracks
wide cement foundation,
building long gone
abandoned wooden rail cars
side lined in tall grassy sidings.
great to climb aboard and dream
whoo, whoo, whoo.

Even a caboose appeared,
left on its way to the bone yard,
with a cabin, bunk beds
where real men might sleep
and a high windowed seat
in the rear to turn
a huge iron wheel
and set the brake,
really something for young
explorers to find!

Piled tracks and rails
here and there in grassy
overgrown heaps
random seeming,
an industrial dump,
rotting ties and waste,
perfect place for weasel,
mink, muskrat,
a rabbit warren
hidden in the past.

We'd hike and hunt,
trap and wander
talking wild talk,
brave and big
upriver, always upriver
toward mythic Saginaw
nine miles north on the line.

On our winter weekends,
we'd set out each journey
filled with enthusiasm,
finishing cold, wet,
but never defeated,
always convinced
just around the next corner
up the line another mile
we'd find a spot where

wilderness began
on the D.M.& I.R. rail line.

It would prove to be
a land that never was,
never will be,
but boys could dream.
Boys could still dream.
Boys will always
dream their dreams.

TEETER TOTTER

Teeter totter,
trees to climb.
We, running wild
screaming.
Forever sunny blue days
hot,
there where the past lives
softening my soul.

We sing shouting
laugh loud
free spinning on the run
gasping out of breath
I won, I won!
as if no force could ever
stop the smiles streaming
from our faces.

Or off to the pond
poking with a stick
at a painted turtle
or carrying a cup to catch
those pollywogs

All in a spring day
just there stuck
deep in my head.
News I need today
in this cold wet April
where my old joints ache.

PARADE, 1959

Every little school
in the county
had a band dressed up
in bright pressed uniforms
to march and play;
celebrate the Fourth of July
with majorettes
and drum majors
high stepping along
ahead, proud.

We always thrilled
as the Cloquet High School band
marched past on the Fourth of July
so quick and proud,
triple time stepping
straight down Cloquet Avenue,
like soldiers themselves
playing the Cloquet fight song
all in rows lead by a drum major,
pennants and flags,
and twirling majorettes.
zooming past
Jefferson School lawn
where we sat on the wall
where we stood on the wall
where we ran out shouting,
how proud we were
when the band

streamed past
at last.

We'd wait and clap
princess this and that,
pretty girls on airy floats
waving languid arms
to wow the crowds
from all the county
around.
We'd applaud
troops and vets
from all the wars;
politicians we did not know
in their fancy cars
old cars, police cars
and flags,
so many flags
big and small
red white blue
banners streaming
confetti all.

It would, seem,
standing in the heat,
that they would never arrive
the last; the best,
marching band ever,
bursting down the avenue.

So much energy and pride
drums beat to quicken the heart.
You had to shout
or run about
laughing such fun.

Years later I played
in that same band
on the Fourth of July,
triple time stepping,
straight down Cloquet Avenue
like a soldier
as proud as I ever imagined,
marching in the Cloquet High School band
could ever be.

Tilt-a-whirl

Jump up
swing in,
slide back,
squiggle wiggle
safety bar set and locked
by that leering guy
with the rude tattoos.

Spin-spun once
then settle down
waiting for all the cars to fill
expectant, so tense
my palms sweaty.
I did not try
to hold yours.

I did not know
how deep feelings ran,
how your eyes
caught my glance;
why my eyes caught yours,
ever drawn together in this
shell of a circus ride
life.

Redwhiteblue,
redwhiteblue
spun so tight
fighting a pull and push,

push and pull
centrifugal teen
attraction
we were as tight
wound as taffy;
one moment
trapped in time,
sweet time.

You me we together
a screaming laughing
tickle me bunch of fun
so, so much fun
surrounded by clinkity clink
wheels whirring
an old nickelodeon played
summer songs in the park

Later, sprawled on the lawn,
hands held soft whispering
watching fireworks
burn sky high
across the baseball diamond
boom kaboom
acrid gun powder smoke.
your soft perfume.

In all the rush
sound and clamor

stood a silence
I can never forget;
a feeling I had never felt before,
and lived in me
forever after.

HIDE AND SEEK

We traced a secret short cut
running, climbing, jumping
through the backyards
around and about our neighborhood.

No one knew but us
where we ran
and hid,
hide and seek.

Along rough brick low walls,
dirt driveways
rickety sheds or behind an old garage
past lilac over grown hedges
lining many of the small lots
between Jefferson School
and our houses
just two blocks up Ninth Street
on the other side of Avenue D.

The only rule I remember now
is that our short cut could never
run on the street side
always had to be hidden
to remain secret
known only the few
who hung on our block.

We were our own

little sect, so
even though Mr. Johnson
saw only a space behind
his garage and
an alley way fence
we knew that space as a hidden track
through dangerous territory
past a snapping yappy Scotty who lived
just next door and barked
if we strayed too close.

From tree to tree,
past backyards and gardens
trash burning barrels
and lost yard junk
we wound our ways.
sometimes off to play
basketball or baseball
in the Jefferson School play lot
where a fence could catch our fouls.

Sometimes just to chase
and run wild
in the summer sun
hiding and seeking,
never really wanting

to lose each other
always just
following the leader
shouting hide and seek.

CRACK THE WHIP

Did you remember to tie
your skates tight?
Wrap those long laces right around the top
so your ankles wouldn't sag
as you thrust around the rink
in flight and flowing,
air whispering through your hair.

So sweet the scene
in nineteen fifty-nine
Lollipop played loud
on that outdoor speaker
lolli, lolli, lolli pop
for you to move
dancing on; slipping
around the rink.

I think,
I was just a little late
rushing to get out of the warming house
knowing full well if I didn't speed
you'd be off spinning
such laugh, dancing fun.
I'd have not a chance to slip
hand in hand round
even once with you
this bright night.

Such a time,
so many fine nights
when we were young.
Snow piles pushed up
sealing the edge
deep and soft.

We would play crack the whip
and yell, oh so loud ,
crash and fall together
these cool winter nights.
Laughing, whooping
winning the world with our zeal
when we were young.

Autumn Night

It's hard to be fifteen
in a small town
in the autumn
when the leaves begin
to drop.

Did I note stars
there in the night sky,
or hear the wind
rushing up through
those oaks and maples
standing past
my bedroom windows,
planted just after the great fire,
now full grown
on the boulevard?

I looked out over
our front yard
sitting on my desktop,
leaning on the windowsill
staring out, lights off,
late night, early autumn
cool sneaking a smoke.

Did I consider the stark beauty,
or just push another puff of smoke
out the window,
hoping old Mrs. Johnson next door

didn't see it rising through the night,
and call Ma to tattle,
say her no good boy
was smoking on the sly
again?

School'd just begun,
every day a challenge
of who's who,
what's what.
no foliage, no hiding spot,
the eyes of the world
upon your every move.
am I cool, am I not?

The stars were stunning bright
against the dark autumn sky
smoke whirling out
an open window,
no one about below.
I see just me and the stars,
and a light breeze
drifting red orange
leaves down to earth.

I wonder if I took the time
to feel the beauty
or just stubbed out
my smoke and went to bed?

It's hard to be fifteen
in a small town
in the autumn
when the leaves begin
to drop.

HUNTING RATS

At nightfall in late August
near the end of boyhood
the Big Lake Road turned south
running along the lake shore.
Fish's Bar was set tucked in
just where a man might need a drink
before moving on,
and a straight old dirt road
set west off into the never-never.

Right up that low woody hill
sat the Big Lake dump,
a pile of old thrown crud,
broken stuff,
yesterday's watermelon rind,
last week's leftovers,
smelling rot,
torn tires, ripped rugs,
an old bed mattress, sprung and wet.
All in a deep heap falling
down the hillside sliding
country dump.

Norwegian rats lived wild
under the lump, moving
after summer's sunset.
They'd skitter out, munch their lunch.
find tonight's treat there at our feet.
We there to hunt rodents.

Fun with a gun.

Flashlights ready, strapped
with black electric tape
on barrel side, a loaded .22
and a shotgun or two.
We slipped out atop the mass
stand still, quiet
waiting long in the dark, very dark
listen, hush,
feel the rats claws rustle
rising, skittering near our feet
at our ankles
crisscrossing here, then there
quiet, so dark quiet
I've never felt such an odd creepy fear
standing near, feeling blind.

Waiting the hushed signal
to click on our flashlights,
sight rats flashing eyes
piercing the dark.

God, what a rush!
Cracking shots
bang, bang, bang,
kaboom.
I still can't imagine
how nobody got shot.

A bloody fun time
loud country fun
loud country
boys becoming men.

DEER CAMP

After dark
a cribbage board
centered an old plank table
set kitchen middle
where hunters
hunkered and bragged.
through a week-long
tournament to see who'd
peg best this season;
who could tell
the tallest tales.

In this kerosene lit,
wood cook stove world,
away from life's clutter
lost in the middle
of the Superior National Forest
a dream for young me
a life for men
hunting off their age.
Camp was their good old days:
tree cruisers, trappers,
choppers, cutters
hunters toasting triumphs
groaning the missed shot
aching the last drive
so alive.

Each morning began lamp lit
over eggs and pancakes
readying the day
rechecking the pack
bullets and knives
match books
a pack of smokes
damp the fire down.
Then huddle over
a map with compasses
we'd plot our course,
hunting as a pack.
some sitting stand
on a section line;
the rest driving
to push the deer out.

Drivers slogged through
mile long strips
side by side
forest and swamp
thick brush, sticks
forcing ourselves on
to prove
we were hunters
If we were lucky
a shot would ring out front
as one of the old men
had his luck.

On the very last day
of this very first hunt,
tired and beaten,
six days,
not a shot taken,
I was standing
at the cabin door
just ready to unload
in the dimming light alone,
when I glanced down
a swampy trail
to see a buck not thirty yards off
walking head down,
sniffing the ground
slowly stepping my way.

It was then I knew
I had a hunter's blood.
With a single shot through his
heart when he looked up
to see me waiting at the door.
that buck entered my heart's eye,
and gave himself,
so that I
could be a man.

They have found me ever since
as I hunt through my autumns,
the deer and I

tied in some cosmic whirl,
where I perform the music
and they join in the dance.

WE, THE CLASS OF 1966

Before I attended
my fiftieth Cloquet High School
class of 1966 reunion,
I wondered aloud who I might see there.
My brother-in-law told me
    "All you're going to see is old people."

He was right.
That's who I saw,
old people, old friends, old loves
Old folks I knew or didn't know
loved, or didn't love,
who brought tears to my eyes,
or flashing, sharp
momentary memories to my mind,
as we recalled our days together
so very, very long ago.

We've lived
the most part of our lives already.
We old folks.
built our dreams
copulated long, long lines of babies,
helped grow babies of babies.
Fought our wars.
Buried our beloved.

Tonight, we old folks
trade worn photos of

Billy and Sally, and
whoever that is standing there
in the middle.

We lined up in long ragged rows
to get our picture taken
by some kid with a camera,
promised immortality in the image.
We ate hearty, laughed loud,
danced a bit.
celebrated our age
our great fortune
our past and present,
future, future perfect.

We congratulated each other
at having managed to reach this age
and our freedom, once getting here
retired.
Our joints ache, our minds slip,
we nap too much and whine
about all those kids piling up below us

We are mostly happy,
mostly satisfied with the way
we've all turned out

We, the Cloquet High School Class of 1966.

III

BECOMING

Pa at Sunrise

I miss you most
mornings
so early even the sun's not risen.
You, quiet, shuffling out
pajama'd, pipe posed,
poised ready in hand.
Silent.

I await a click.
Snapped match
struck against
that old wood armed chair,
or to hear you rattle
through the cupboard
muttering short dream confusions,
brewing up your first cup,
firing the stove
to burn off
another night's chill.

And I,
focusing my eyes barely
burst through evening's dreams
awakening,
I wait
and follow the progress
of your day, celebrating
how well I know
what it is I cannot see.

It was
always still
always silent
always peaceful
always quiet
except for your small intrusions,
preparations.

It was then we'd talk
hushed not to waken the day:
about the rooster's early rise
or the state of the nation
or the wood pile's size
or your health
or my future
our day's plan
progress
related.

Tied there to who we were
and where we were,
your eyes resting lightly
affirming
my place
as I answered and asked
in my best good son's voice,
boy once again.

You would ask me how I was

and I would say,
(in so many words),
fine,
without guilt
knowing
that I could not say other
to an old man
on an early sunny day
in the summer in the middle
of another short visit
home.

How could I tell you
how unsure I was
or how my pain gained with time
or how confused my life had become
or how I felt frustrated,
insufficient, angry,
Or how I wished forever
for your peace of mind?
I didn't, couldn't
wouldn't disturb your dream of me,
your approval
of my life away from
your great plain ideals.

Your good son was asea,
facing his challenges with triumph
and heady with young

strong dreams.
It could not be me
muddling my life,
not me, you could not see
in our veiled darkness.

I could not ask your council then
or your confessional now.

Gloom intrudes
its mist on my vision now.
Though I still await your speculations
and revelations,
too late
to grasp the thread of what it was
you held
that I cannot find,

or at least,

I listen for the soft shuffle of your feet
searching a calm moment,
a robin singing high early,
before the wind rises
gazing as I do now
out the long
tide line.

LEARNING TOOLS

Pa taught me
to whittle a stick
holding blade
directed away,
always pacing the stroke,
working broken branch
in paper thin slivers
fluttering at my feet
into something I could use.
knife haft gripped tight
bracing branch well
low against my knee,
focusing on the cut.

Never let the blade slip
or twist deep in the grain
carve a polished point.
Let the wind in the trees
course through my arm
working, working, working
the wood.

So I shaped a new tool
under my father's watchful eye
used to roast a wiener over the fire
that was lit earlier in the day,
when I was out diving
off the raft out front
and Mom set the yard

for dinner.

Later to roast a marshmallow
rolling it carefully over
the embers as the night sky
filled with stars
and we laughed as
our treats burst into flame
blow, blow, blow
the flame out
and
wait, wait, wait,
or you'll burn your tongue,
lips, teeth,
so sweet.

Mom's Song

An age of hands rung,
songs sung at the sink
getting another night's
dishes done
wondering where
time, time, time's
come and gone
long, long gone.

I still hear her voice
singing light show tunes,
Broadway hits,
whispered, hummed
high and light
there looking out her bay window
in the evening sun setting
wrinkles smoothed
on her old brow
now the kids were
all left home
grown and gone.

Music hummed
around her work
a perpetual background
cooking, sewing, cleaning,
mop in hand
a whirl wind homemaker,
knitter, baker,

busy mom.

She even sang sewed
that lost fallen button eye
back onto Teddy's head
for me not to worry
never worry.
my mom
come and gone
long, long gone.

COAL SPACE HEATER

A coal space heater works pretty well
in a two-story house if it is
placed right under the vent hole
cut 12 X 12 through the living room ceiling
to the second floor bedroom

Through it a boy could hear
the night pass
after being sent up to bed.
Just by pushing a little lever
there, on the side,
it opened and closed,
tin flaps like Venetian blinds,
allowing heat
from the old coal heater
to rise through,
or not.

The clink and clang
of dishes washed in the kitchen,
there the icebox opens and closes
or the back storm door
banged with a snap.
A way to extend the day,
keep track of the night life world
with all the heat a boy might want.
Hearing Mom, Dad and the older kids
up listening to the radio
or playing cards,

or the sound of snoring
from the couch below.

All my world there running below
but a boy must be quiet
so as not to be heard
slipping in and out of bed,
sliding to the vent
stockinged, walking quiet.
Sometimes at sunrise
I'd awaken on the floor
huddled by the vent
in dim light
cheek pressed tight waiting.

Root Cellar

You don't understand.

You got into the root cellar
through a trap door
right in the middle of the kitchen
floor.
Imagine that!
Below the kitchen table,
between the stove and the fridge,
right beside the sink
was a metal latch.

You lifted it
to get to the stairs
leading down into the cellar:
first you moved the table out of the way
then lifted a heavy wood door
hinged into the floor
leaned it up against the far wall
and stretched down
to click on a strung light
hung on the cellar ceiling beam.

Sometimes you could imagine small eyes
or hear a rustle
way down there below.
A steep stairway
jumped five steps down
to the dirt floor below.

Potato bins behind the stair,
shelves to each side and back,
all stacked neatly.
Canned peaches and beans
and peas and berries
every other thing our family
ate through winter into spring.

It was musty and damp
low ceilinged,
hard to see into the corners
scary, very scary.
No place for a boy to be alone.

STRAWBERRIES

As a child holding
my mother's hand
I picked berries,
snuck a few to eat,
and watched the ants
on a hot June day,
knowing sweet,
sharp juices would soon
run past my tongue.

I listened to bees and bugs.
jumped the cow pies,
in Heikala's cow pasture
where just enough berries grew
to make a short cake
if we were diligent
and allowed nature to push us on.

My lips turned bright red
as we picked
She teased me
and I promised not to eat any more.
As the afternoon wore on,
my eyes
drifted quietly closed.
I lay down in soft grasses
near her berry cup.

It was an age ago,
that quiet memory.
still resting in my brain
stuck sweet and peace filled
as my mother's gentle touch
woke me and carried me home.

Canning

In August it seemed
every homemaker
in the Upper Midwest
canned peaches,
lots of peaches
with a few pears
thrown in.

Whole train loads
of fresh fruit picked in orchards
where fruits other than apples
grew on brightly colored trees
wild, foreign states
like Georgia, Florida,
Alabama, California,
arrived at our door.

We, ma and me,
we stood in the heat
of an afternoon gas stove kitchen
boiling pots of water,
scalding the skins off peaches,
plunging them into icy sink baths,
peeling the cooled skins off
(Gently, don't bruise the fruit),
revealing slippery smooth
flesh below, fragrant,
sweet smelling ripe fruit.
scalding, peeling, plunging.

We sliced the fruit,
split off the pit,
squeezed each half
into a well washed
Ball quart jar,
filled with syrup half inch
below the rim,
then capped, banded
each five-quart batch
immersed in boiling water
20 minutes for safe keeping.

Cooled on racks
lined up like soldiers
all in formation
all in a row...
You'd hear the metallic snap
as they sealed
one at a time.
A ping unlike any other
in a young boy's life.

Half a case of pears
canned as an after thought
all shelved with the blueberries, raspberries
apples picked local,
wild out in the country
where fallen farmsteads
left them for us to find.

Enough fruit for a family of five
to stretch through the winter months
stored cool and dark
below the kitchen floor in that old root cellar
dug and lined with shelves
before even the house went up
after the great fire
in the winter of 1919.

BLUEBERRY PIE

Jesus it was hot,
in that thick syrupy air,
heat waves rising
off low swampy plots
strewn about those
ancient river bottoms,
deep in July.

My family gathered
out picking right by the railroad grade
dressed in long pants,
sleeved shirts,
brimmed hats worn low
bandanas around our necks
searching for
blueberries by the bucket
Ma said, "easy pickins."

Wet, dirty,
sweat running down.
horse flies, deer flies, red ant hills
mosquitoes, yellow jackets,
spiders big and small
could not run me away.
Those deer flies so quick,
one hand swatting,
while the other picked
eyes always focused
on the next good bush,

there, up ahead
blue, grey, more green blue
bushes.

So still, quiet
but the buzz of the bugs.
Rocks a million years resting
dark, looming up,
I crouched picking in a great river's channel
once rushing south to the sea
in the strikes and scars carved
where blueberries now grew lush.

Under that hot July sun
vision blurred by sweat and bugs
was Ma's hot blueberry deep dish pie,
a sweet scoop of vanilla ice cream,
wedged tight in my brain,
but
that damned gallon can
strung to my waist
filling with the slow patter of berries
raining down,
seemed to never quite
topped up to the brim.

Later, sitting on the back porch,
as Ma made that first fresh picked pie
we sifted over the berries,

pouring them out
on spread newspapers,
skimming leaves and bugs
proofing our harvest clean,
making them ready for table or jar
then waited call to supper
and the earned release
of hot blueberry deep dish pie
on a sunny summer evening in July
laughter and chatter
until sun set.
A good day to be alive.

Good Baked Bread

The key to good risen bread
is in the yeast
that bare, grainy beginning
of all that comes next.

Set to swell
under the morning light
sugar water on our stove
made the dough rise just right.

an ability to read the signs,
weather, light of day
feel of the work in your hands,
takes a bursting drive
and love of where the yeast leads.

My recipes were all learned young
at my mother's side where she threw together
this and that
flour, scalded milk, Crisco, salt
simple.

I felt the dough smooth in her hands
and heard her sing as she worked
(old Broadway standards)
kneading the dough slow steady
hearing her push away, and turn
push and turn
to the sway of some old tune.

She let me taste the progress
the tensile strength
I learned to know how the dough
must feel at first
and last before it rose,
and rose, and molded to shape
then entered the oven
hot.

I could not forget that
even if I knew how now
nor would I
so fixed are those moments in my mind
like glass in a window.
I see me
learning the smell, tastes, feel
of the day, as I replicate it now
this half century later
looking back.

Rain Barrel

A light June rain is falling
this eleventh day
after a week of dry,
dripping off the eaves
channeled gutters above
washing away
on the sidewalk,
driveway
green grassy edge
washing away.

When I was a boy
we had a barrel
at the base
of a down spout
to catch the rush
from each spring storm
save for later.
Once I rescued a frog
bobbing fallen off the edge
carefully put it back
in those lilies of the valley
where it obviously belonged

Barreled rainwater
fed my mother's gardens,
she said,
rainwater pleases peonies,
tastes of rainbow,

soft and sweet.

I believe that is true.
but I have no barrel
out back to save
the rain today
for tomorrow's drought
another kindness lost.
My peonies
will live their lives
on bought water.
I wonder if they are
as bright as my mother's,
sipping rainbows
each day?

Wood Nymph

Lying on a dark mossy rock
well off the shore of a silent lake,
up there in the boundary waters
on a hot summer day,
when I was still young enough
to believe in a little magic,
I rested in the middle
of a heavy fir grove,
the only opening
hidden but at midday
with a high sun.

I listened to the flies buzzing past me
there in the heat,
smelling sweet cedar,
eyes closed,
face brushing the soft mosses
slowly drifting
off into dreams.

Then came a light crack,
a rustle and,
raising one eye, slowly, I saw
not ten feet off out of reach
just at the base of my rocky perch
a doe fawn sniffing the air.

Tentative
stretching one front hoof

up, down curious,
trembling, watching
up at me.
I dared not move
an inch for a bit.

But, out of wonder,
I lifted my head merely that inch,
she, so startled, jumped off
into a breach in the woods.
Gone in a white flash. Gone.

When I walked back to camp
later, to tell my tale,
none of the kids believed me.
I was always making things up
there in the woods. True.
Sometimes now, I still do.

JALONEN'S FARM

There was a pig
who lived on Jalonen's farm
just up the hill from our cabin,
and down the drive
at the very end past the poppy rows
and a steep mowed lawn
that ran down to the beach
where their sauna stood.
We would steam
on a summer's eve
to sweat grime
and worries away.

Later we'd climb to stand
by their barn where
a rough-cut grey wood pen
held a being of great bulk,
to talk with Mr. Pig.

I, draped in a towel
still warm and wet haired
as the sun set down
under the wailing loons' calls,
and humahum of a million frogs,
echoing off over our bay
ending another summer day
at the lake

He grunting loud

and rooting as I stood
his small darting eyes
looking right at me
eye to eye were we,
the pig and me.

I was brave about it,
asked how he was doing,
watched as he ate
and snuffed
just like you'd expect a pig to be.
Big, rough skinned, muddy.
hungry, always hungry
was he.

He was the first and last pig
I ever knew well enough
to address as Mr. Pig.
In autumn he was gone
We never talked about
his passing.

Swing

Back then
my home wore white walls,
dark green trimmed window frames.
It was open porched
from side to side.
A big dark wooden door center,
opened into the living room
with two steps leading up
and a tin lidded box for milk
sitting by its side.

In the north corner hung
a dark green slat wood swing
hung from creaky chains
you'd hear whenever someone rocked
even a little bit
crick, creek-a-creek, crick
on a summer's eve at sunset.

There were vines
that ran along the rails
up the side pillars
to eaves edge,
my parents wanted them gone.
I don't now know why
perhaps I never did.

It was an old house
built after the great fire

when all the old houses
in all the town
were built again
1919 reborn.

I walked past the other day
just to see,
recognize a place I had been
when my world was small and fresh,
discovering the porch walled over,
fully enclosed.
No doubt the swing gone
No doubt, no one but me
remembers the creek-a-creek
on a summer's eve anymore.

Does that matter,
if when I dream
of soft summer nights
and the whispers
of my mother and father
talking softly in the cool
evening air,
where the swing hung
and what it said,
as long as I was there?

THANKSGIVING

I am thankful
mother taught me the golden rule
early in life.
I have done
(mostly) unto others
ever since,
and they have done
(mostly) the same unto me.
I know that kindness counts.

I am thankful
that dad taught me to persevere
and fight through
by living example
as the shifts piled
on his old soul.
He taught me to not quit,
and I never quit. Not easily.

I am thankful
for all the people
who are my friends and family
and my students
and my teachers
for all the good lessons
and joy
they brought to my door.

I am thankful
I finally learned to learn
and listen,
and to lead with my heart.

I am thankful
for my age
and for my bounty,
having led a simple life
without much fuss.

I am thankful
for the patience of others
and their small kindnesses
that have given me solace
in those times when I fell.

I am thankful
for finding unending life
and love hidden here
right where I left it.

There is little in life
that is not a blessing of some kind;
some bumps are a little rough,
but once you get by them,
smooth waters lie ahead.
smooth waters
always lie ahead.

WISHBOOK

It is the lights at night…
a glow on the snow.
nowhere else on earth
dragged the merry out
so well as the wishbook.

When I was young
Montgomery Ward's catalog
inches thick; heavy,
sparkled my eyes
every November
circus sounding
something fun,
colorful toys, games
to page through
fold corner,
fold corner,
fold corner down.

A boy's subtle hint
where good stuff
would be found.
then wait and wish:
erector set
BB gun,
fortress, soldiers
knights in armor
electric train
bow and arrows

new sled, skis
bike or skates
bright shiny wishes
all for me.

Days grew short, darker.
Dad put up a Christmas tree
to light our way
through years end.
when finally my
wishes would be filled,
wrapped in shiny bright paper,
hid under a brilliant tree.

In our ancient past
we lived by firelight
these long nights,
trees burst with sap
lit, fired to drive away dark.

You can almost hear echoes
of drummers and chants
calling across lakes, forests,
dancing up the sun
one step and again.
driving winter down
from the winter woods.

In this season now
I hold not a wishbook
not a flame, nor do I dance
around a fire.
Instead, I will away
these darkest days,
recalling a child's dream,
songs, and stories,
paging through days.
each a piece
of the same frame:
remembrance, celebration
wish willing the dark away
songs and dances,
around fires in the night
gifts you can barely imagine.

CHRISTMAS

I have made
the cookies, candy,
sweet, special breads.
set the table filled
with the best of the best,
waiting patient for the coming
but still you have gone.
It isn't death I fear,
but the living,
moving on.

I've placed festive trees,
decorated sparkling,
Santa, candles, yule log
snow globes set about.
cards lined up across mantles
stockings hung high.

Colorful lighted bulbs
cover outdoor decks
and all along the eaves
poinsettias red and pink.
amaryllis in full bloom.
all the makings of fine celebrations
with pageants and songs.

So I wait the night.
the rise of the moon.
the coming of all the magic,

just as it has come
every other year
and still you are gone.
It isn't death I fear,
but the living,
moving on.

The Things We Lost

The things we left behind
disposable; replaceable
trampled,
a long, long trail:

clothes pins coat hangers
plastic container covers
loves hates
earrings paper clips
photographs receipts,
canceled checks
rubber gaskets
six penny nails
screws ambitions,
chunks of pipe
hasps locks passions
broken hammers
window glass note paper
socks memories reasons
spice bottles tacks, tape
telephone directories
tools toys
books books and books.
All equal parts
of our lives left,
new lives beginning
on, always on.

But the vision of who we were

where we were going,
how crucial it was to arrive,
alive
always stayed with us
stories, legends,
waiting to for us to look back,
see the trail behind,
and venture
where we had been
begin again.

IV

DISTANCE

VI

Distance

Winter Red Squirrel

That red squirrel living
in our gazebo,
is making it
his (maybe her)
own home,
though bent, old
and leaning a bit with age.
I see sun flower seed shells
scattered here and there
on the floor and ledges
when I go to scoop
a bucket of seed to feed
the winter birds
flocking in our backyard.

I suspect,
she (maybe he)
plans a family,
to take root under
its old plank floor,
where piled up planting pots,
propped shovels and rakes make
good climbing for young squirrels to learn
how to traverse the world mid air
or run up the wall, around the screen,
and down below to nest.

Now and again we spy each other;
me from the sliding glass living room door

as I close and lock up for the night, and
he (maybe she)
sitting on an inner wall ledge
at the screen's edge
watching slyly, warily out at me
to see what it is I might be doing
in my snug house as
she (maybe he)
huddles, eating a good last seed,
before curling up below the floor
warm as
he (maybe she)
can be
wrapped up in squirrel fur,
perfectly safe and secure,
beneath my winter stored
barbecue grill and
fifty-gallon galvanized drum
filled full with seed.

We have a truce
she (maybe he)
and me,
this cold winter season.
When summer comes on,
the air warms, and days grow long,
I will expect
him (maybe her)
to move on,

and
he (maybe she)
will expect to stay.

It could make for a long,
long squirrely summer.
I think
she(maybe he)
considers this gazebo is
a great place to raise
a family. I think it not.

Slow Dancing

The walk is best done
wearing comfortable shoes
in early morning
before mosquitoes and gnats
fill our river valley
summers,
and in winter
on sunny days
before the crusted snow melts
making a slippery walk along this path
toward town.

Geese, swans and ducks
gather below
plunging for fallen wild rice seed
into the cool water,
icy water,
frozen water
every season of the year.

Occasional otters meet
in the beds to feed
on fingerling fishes
during spring;
in autumn
you can hear red winged blackbirds,
thousands,
squawk through the rice stalks.
berries and mushrooms and leaves

all feed something to someone
here on river's edge.

There is no creature
that does not gather
near the rice beds,
all of them
looking for a take-out menu,
or simple dessert tray,
a reason to extend their lovely stay,
after last night's slow dance
with the moon.
Just a few more bites
before moving on.

As I am,
after last night's slow dance,
that near moment when
only we,
in all the world, mattered,
wanting to extend the moon's glow
just a second more,
standing at river's edge
the sun's rise
my food
before moving on.

WINTERING

We winter well
here north
within our dark days,
short, ever shorter,
long cold nights,
so crisp the stars stand
upon us cold,
as their lights flicker
sparkling the snow.
It is quiet now.
The earth is closed,
huddled, nested,
waiting spring.

There lies a great poplar
toppled this past summer,
storm blasted,
root ball wrestled loose,
now sinking back to earth,
a great long pale
monster tree stretched out
along the forest floor.
Becoming food
for mosses, lichen,
beetles, and birds,
gathering now
to celebrate its demise,
feast, build great colonies
within, without this new home

born of wind and gravity safe.
a metamorphic rest,
feeding lives through to spring.

Tracks along the forest floor
tell me that other life
too lives winter differently
through these dark days.
That plump bear cub,
born a year past
fattened on berries, fish,
acorns summer long,
who I tracked down
a wooded October trail.
He is now hid beneath,
denned in a world of dreams
more better for him
than winter's
stark earth.

He saves the future
as winter goes
in fantastic slumber
this season away
deep beneath
sheltering snow,
carrying life
through to spring,

as we of the North
will carry another year
past its last full moon,
its most short day,
its most long night,
and wait the rising
spring flood.

All Around Me

I see birth and death
death and birth
all again working
beginning and ending
dark then light.
A path circling our earth
each season a new start, finish,
plant then harvest,
begin and end.

The cycle never stops
nor would the moon allow it
nor the sun,
or the tides
or the wind
or clouds floating high
or bowing trees
or growing grasses
on which we walk.
All is motion.

We have danced
this song for eons,
for ages, forever.
Nature is in us;
it holds us
it is us

asking only that we step
into its flow and
wiggle our toes
to feel the magic.

CHOICES

If I were a strong man
I would have done other with my life
than feed the children their daily pap
and watch them grow through my classroom,
or ponder the ideas of others
as if I could have none of my own.

Or I would have built large things
to clutter other people's lives
and filled them with my confusion
watching as they bought my dreams
filling their heads with who I was
and what I thought today.

Or traveled far and wide
and reported on my amazing perceptions
telling tales of what I saw
and what I had done
and how important that was to all
who might see how I had seen.

But it was never me to be
outstanding from the rest,
hidden.
I have been feeling my life
slip past, knowing
here I sit,
with my dreams still

trapped in my being
no longer running the race.

Today,
I want only to be me,
hold my own counsel,
fulfill my own dreams
manage what future remains,
resolved and set.
In that, I am strong.

.

ARTIFACTS

In the strata left
by this age of man
compressed
driven deep
arisen again
making a slip
fault in some far away
mountain range.
What simple shard will teach
the lessons
we humans learned
and left?

The laws we wrote
or laws we broke.
Where will be we,
the right and just,
rest in the narrowed
rubble we've left?

Diamonds do not sparkle much
on the long fingers of time
nor musical chords or
all the lovely art,
audacious acts,
brilliant finds,
opera, music, stage.
crafts and skills,
all smears; mere

stains on the rock.

Our leering gestures
at innocence,
lusts, and ire,
our damned arms and wars
will be there
just dust.

AFTERLIFE

I have seen death enter my home
sneaking through a deep night door
hidden, stealthy
like a mist shrouded silent

Oh, I do not fear it.
Death is a passing,
a dream path unknown,
like that fairy story I told you
once upon a time
when the night was late
and we lay awake
listening
to frogs harrumph off the lake
loons chuckling high and long
all down the shore
so hot we could not sleep
atop our feathery beds.

Once upon a time long, long ago
when elves still walked the earth,
I wove stories to make your eyes close
drifting off, drift off, drift off.

Once upon a time
I wove princesses and kings
soldiers, lovers, and dragons,
all in all for you
while death entered our home

sneaking in the deep night door
hidden, stealthy
as a mist
shrouded silent,

so in your last moments
on earth wrapped in my arms,
I told a tale
weaving a place just here
in my heart for you,
once upon a time.

STATUARY

We are made of the earth
in an everlasting dance.

Love is surely
wrapped in stone
just as we all
will be cast in stone
somewhere, someday,
someway churned
apart, together.
forever.

Metamorphic,
igneous,
sedimentary
limestone, sandstone
granite, marble, chert
held tight
holding lives
once lived
never alone.

Fallen leaves
wind tripped trees
bones long buried
old everything
molded by
rushing rivers
tide lines

volcanic thrusts
drifted sand dunes
mudded water
pushed up dust
scraped by great glaciers
through dawns and dusks
all a motion,
all emotion.

Held tight
to begin again
each autumn, spring
winter, summer
so green and bursting
young, vibrant
wailing running wild
hands held swinging
embracing the light
of a new day,
new lease
on life and love
every morn for eons
every eon in eternity.
we are made of the earth
in an everlasting dance.

Patrick Stevens is a lifelong teacher, nature lover, and writer.

Upon graduation from the University of Minnesota in 1974, Stevens taught high school English in Grygla, Minnesota. He migrated to Sitka, Alaska, in 1977 where he taught language arts in the public schools and later at the University of Alaska. In 2002 he returned to Minnesota, working as librarian and education director for the Minnesota Department of Corrections. He retired in 2008.

Panning Gold is his first published book of poetry, celebrating life growing up in a small, midwestern American town prior to the mid-1960's. The poems focus on that experience and on the lives of townspeople during that era.

Patrick Stevens lives in northeastern Minnesota in the company of his two cairn terriers, Sadie Mae and SamIam.

ACKNOWLEDGMENTS

I would not have completed this collection without the support of Tim Jollymore and Kathleen Stamm who appeared at just the right time and gave me a kick in just the right place. Their insistence, skills and effort made the book happen.

P.S.